Songs from the Underground

poems

by

Caitlin M.S. Buxbaum

Red Sweater Press
P.O. Box 870414
Wasilla, AK 99687
caitbuxbaum.com/red-sweater-press

Copyright © 2019 Caitlin M.S. Buxbaum. All rights reserved.

Printing fulfilled by Amazon. No part of this book may be used or reproduced in any manner whatsoever without written permission of the publisher except in the case of brief quotations embodied in critical articles and reviews.

All included images are the work of the author.

ISBN-13: 978-1-7332677-1-7
ISBN-10: 1-7332677-1-9

For my parents

Contents

Fomented Etheree	1
Ruined Lullaby	2
Your Poem	3
Seven (Happy Birthday)	4
At the Pulpit	6
Despair	8
The Sphinx Moth	9
Imperfect Pantoum	10
To Su Smallen	12
When Uncle Brad was an Elf	13
Unsound Sonnet	14
Sonnetto	15
Paper Football	16
The God Balloon	18
He knows the subtleties of how she runs	20
Pie Eating Contest	21
The Fall	22
First Fruits	24
Inhibition	25
Johnny-Be-Good	27

About the Author

Songs from the Underground

Fomented Etheree

What
is it
that form does
for poetry
to make it at once
infuriating and
also the most priceless work
of art the self composes, in
the heat of the moment or in cold
calculation, to speak the truth of thought?

Ruined Lullaby

in the sleepy haze of 6 a.m.
crowfeet tapping on a tin roof
sounds like lullaby-water,
bubble-dripping into my dreams
beside shimmering onyx feathers

but under the smell-weight
of three-days-worth of eggs,
                  onions,
                      sweat, and
                        fresh papaya,
feet become *talons*, scraping like nails
on a chalkboard, crippled by the macabre stigma
of black-winged reapers

I wish I had a fucking stone
to silence the racket
of my ruined lullaby.

Your Poem

Read in the wived meter and rhyme
with your voice, this poem's not mine,
though I'll re-write it once or twice.
In reading, your meter and rhyme
will wive my writing once or twice
to your voice (poetic noise), not mine.
Woven red through meter and rhyme:
your vocal threads, poetry not mine.

Seven (Happy Birthday)

I made my grandfather a birthday card
for his seventy-seventh: July 7th, 2007.
I thought it was lucky.

I imagined him opening it — sorry, Gran'pa,
I hope you don't mind that my gift
is the same as last year: another wrinkle
at each corner of your mouth, some more
near your eyes. Sorry, Gran'pa, that revenge
got the better of me for that brown cow joke:

> *You know that chocolate ice cream*
> *comes from brown cows, don't you?*

I didn't know you were lying, but
I laughed in wonder and licked the chocolate
off my face anyway. I still smile.

So, you win, Gran'pa, still carving those lines
in my face, I no longer able to in yours.
Happy birthday anyway

At the Pulpit

I am like a child
viewing your paint-chipped palms
with *hair*-brained ideas in my head
weaving down my backbone
into a creative core

Are you inspired? I ask
in my "spirit voice,"
staring up at the preacher.
Is that why you are painted,
like me?

I watch the hairs on his arms
not move
where the plain-colored flecks
are stuck.

No, creation is more colorful,
I say, again in silence.
You must not be inspired
today.

Despair

Four miles from home,
I can hear the hunchback crows
cawing in the cemetery,
where I'm bound to be buried
after this, with a headstone reading:
        RAN TO DEATH.
Deep down,
I know it isn't possible (today),
but I roll to a stop and push
my fingers through the earth
for a drink of water.

The Sphinx Moth

Soft bodies of birds
or bees; never holding still
enough to know which

Within Shakespeare's Dream
or Carroll's Wonderland may
be hummingbirds with

six legs each hover
ring around the posy-ground
stick noses in your

father's business—mine,
at least, though fur or feather
becomes less—mottled

not like fish, but swim
through swift-blown wind for just one
September evening

Imperfect Pantoum

I saw a college girl, straight-backed, riding
a bicycle, skirt flowing astride it,
as she slowly pedaled by. Gracefully,
she sat enslaved to fashion upon that

old bicycle, her skirt flowing astride it.
And yet, so peaceful, she seemed to sit, not
enslaved to fashion, but more in subtle
defiance of "traditional values."

And yet, so peaceful, she indeed was not
supportive of passivity, watching
reliance on "traditional values"
shape the reality in which she rode.

Supportive of silent dissent, I watched
the wheels of her bony bicycle spin
and shape reality with her abode,
the synthesis of mind, soul and body

as wheels turn today's political spin
on everyday behavior and action
back to human basics: mind, soul, body.
The ungendered whimsy disappears.

Every day now, my behavior, actions,
and thoughts revolve around man and woman,
two human "basics" in mind, soul, body.
Are we who we are? Well, I bet she knows.

To Su Smallen

Fine.
Defy the laws of poetry
if you must. But do you think
your poems are prosier,
or less prose-y
with the italics and the foreign words,
the fake epigraphs and randomly repeated alliteration,
and the backslashes used for irrational   line breaks
but not for
pauses
or essay citations?
Mostly, I assume
your poems are simply stream of consciousness, going and going and
going
as if words, by extending   the lines   long enough,
would reach your audience / with more understanding.

But then I remember that sometimes,
we like the sounds of words
and the looks of mind-images
enough to forget
the billboard-portrait of genius we expect,
and let our love of language maNIPuLAtion
carry us away
on a sea of nonsensical
dreaming.

When Uncle Brad was an Elf

We thought he'd had his ears surgically altered. I think my mom was already resigned to the fact that her second older brother was strange, but when he ambled up the driveway with pointy ears and a velvet vest with no shirt underneath, everyone hoped—and didn't hope—that someone would explain not the elephant, but the elf in the room. Sometime between dinner and the family photo, it came out that even Texans have hippies and fairy conventions in forests that provide Woodstock-style entertainment. Uncle Brad assured us that his elfin features were merely products of rubber and Super Glue, but I think my great aunt Carol's furtive glances across the dinner table or over the back of the sofa said that his explanation left something to be desired.

In a guitar shop the following afternoon, watching my uncle strum up a band of strangers in his poor-man clothes, a whimsical smile on his face, I let the folksy music fill my ears while I pictured the phantom prongs of his: an image of sharp wit gone dull in his family's eyes.

Unsound Sonnet

There's a little bird outside my window
fluttering spooked in the ivy,
that to the warmth of my most humble room
alone its wing'd mind is privy
to the rhythm of resounding lines
of sonnets read too quickly,
while Shakespeare's words sickly tumble forth
with less mast'ry than folly.
That you, O unbefitted creature'd fly
to some fair and better-spoken poet,
I urge thee onward; be yet far away
from I who to thee so deeply owest
    inspiration's subtle wanderings
    amidst absent-minded ponderings.

Sonnetto

—remove yourself from me, little bird,
to whom I owe this debt: inspiration
from ponderings. There in the ivy,
you've buried yourself
to hear my fattened tongue
taint wiser words from men of fame
by the rhythm of your solitary wings,
and my empty-headed room—empty,
save one, which only bids you hasten
away, far from that unsound window
to poetry's softer mouth.

Paper Football

One, two, three, four,
five, six folds and a seventh
from the opposite end, plus an eighth
back on itself to form a triangle
tucked or shoved
into place, depending on the foresight
and patience of its maker
and also the medium:
a gum wrapper quietly manipulated,
construction paper roughly handled,
or a math assignment long past "relevant"
to the mischievous fingers
setting up their fleshy field goal,
awaiting the punt.

The God Balloon

Low tire pressure or a rough patch
of pavement has me reaching
for the God balloon,
just long enough
for a quick prayer
before the highway
disappears

Funny,
that the twenty-seven
memorial wreaths, make-shift crosses and RIPs
don't question
the inflation of death
described in the faces imprinted on airbags;
I wonder

how many of those hands
sought that feeble string anchor
in desperation,
clinging hopefully to Earth, yet
still imagining
the sound of their lifeline
popping

and why is it
that there aren't more of us
who welcome annihilation,
forget the rubber ideal of convenience
that the world gifted us,
and delight
to meet our maker?

As civilization comes into view,
my palms unclench from the steering wheel,
my knuckles un-whiten against the black leather,
my fingers peel back slowly
in wary but willful obedience to destiny, and
I release the God Balloon—

I am not alone.

The God Balloon

Low tire pressure or a rough patch
of pavement has me reaching
for the God balloon
just long enough
for a quick prayer
before the highway
disappears

Funny,
that the twenty-seven
memorial wreaths, make-shift crosses, and RIPs
don't question
the inflation of death
described in the faces imprinted on airbags;
I wonder

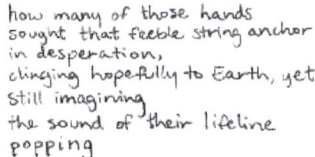

how many of those hands
sought that feeble string anchor
in desperation,
clinging hopefully to Earth, yet
still imagining
the sound of their lifeline
popping

and why is it
that there aren't more of us
who welcome annihilation,
forget the rubber ideal of convenience
that the world gifted us,
and delight
to meet our maker?

As civilization comes into view,
my palms unclench from the steering wheel,
my knuckles un-whiten against the black leather,
my fingers peel back slowly
in wary but willful obedience to destiny, and
I release the God Balloon —

I am not alone.

He knows the subtleties of how she runs

He knows the subtleties of how she runs:
her preference for the inside lane,
the kick that comes a quarter-mile too soon,
and the suddenly blank look in her eyes
that means she's about to throw an elbow
that only he and the girl on the other team
will notice —

but that's just racing. In practice,
there's the head-tilt she starts
when she needs him
to yell at her, and the angry break-away
that means she needs to run alone,
not that she's actually mad
at him.

Sometimes it's just the two of them,
fading into the paved distance
with even strides to match
their mutual goal: endure. At times like these,
she lets him watch her blonde ponytail
swing stubbornly out of sync
with the rhythm of her steps,
without judgment.

He knows the subtleties of how she runs.

Pie Eating Contest

You put your pudding face on
with no rhyme or reason,
only taste to your name;
so lonely but so willing
to be smeared.
                    It's not like you
to be so forgiving, she said,
only cowards await the dawn
without dessert.
Fat with cheating, you look
to Walt Whitman for solace
and find only remorse
at having sacrificed your body
for the will of the people,
and not your own sticky goodness.

The Fall

someone forgot to pick up the kids
after school:
Mom and Dad yell,
daughter cries,
son hides,
everyone goes to their rooms.

First Fruits

Pear juice falls from my lips
like rain in December—cold and uninviting
on my bare thighs, naked from heated sleep
under the safety of my winter blanket

still, no less inspiring than
the first fruits of any morning.
I hurry to wipe up the leakage
before it sinks into my skin,
forever bound inside my body.

Inhibition

in response to Rita Dove's "Flirtation"

But then, why not make
the scene complete

with touch; a garden traced
by fingers sparked

with familiar desire in secret
Everything is new.

Inside the heart
quails before the mind

and "reason" creeps
over the brain. My soul

is afflicted by
what I have never known!

Self-doubt's cruel ploy —
we'll hide and wonder.

"There are ways
to make of the moment"

a commentary,
and the danger's in

excessive thought.

Johnny-Be-Good

Well, my Johnny done right by me,
my Johnny, he done me good
But by good ol' Uncle Sam,
young Johnny ain't done like 'e should.

Johnny-be-good, Johnny-be-good,
Johnny-be-good's been bad today.

Johnny-be-good, Johnny-be-good,
Johnny-be-good's been bad today.

So Johnny, my guy, he run
young Johnny took off, 'e did
To keep away from Uncle Sam,
my Johnny, he ran and hid.

Johnny-do-good, Johnny-do-good,
Johnny-do-good's done bad today.

Johnny-do-good, Johnny-do-good,
Johnny-do-good's done bad today.

Oh to God I sent my prayer,
I said, 'Lord, send us a flood
To wash away that dirty war
and save me my Johnny-be-good.'

God, ye been good, God, ye been good,
God, please be good to my Johnny today.

God, ye been good, God, ye been good,
God, please be good to my Johnny today.

Well, the Lord, 'e 'eard my prayer,
the Lord, 'e sent us a flood
But tho' Johnny 'scaped hard Uncle Sam
he done got dead for good.

My Johnny's blood — Johnny-be-good's —
my Johnny's blood on my hands today.

My Johnny's blood—Johnny-do-good's—
my Johnny's blood on my hands today.

Oh Johnny, I'm sorry, you know
poor Johnny, I killed you dead
I took your love—you gave it so good
your grave was dug here in our bed.

Johnny-be-good, Johnny-be-good,
Johnny-be-good gone to heaven today.

Johnny-be-good, Johnny-be-good,
Johnny-be-good gone to heaven today.

Y'know, Johnny ain't killed
no man, no woman, no child
But if love be a sin, oh
Hell, we're all done in.

Acknowledgments

Thank you to Joyce Sutphen, my illustrious poetry professor, and every other teacher that encouraged me in English Language Arts. At Gustavus: Florence Amamoto, Elizabeth Baer, Phil Bryant, Sean Cobb, Rebecca Fremo, Rob Kendrick, Baker Lawley, Sun Hee Lee and So Young Park; at Colony High: Susan Brunner, Kelly Kuzina, Prudence Plunkett and Kelly Thaler; at Colony Middle: Judith Darling, Emily Forstner and Dan Klauder; and at Snowshoe Elementary: Vanessa Powell and Holly Sharrow.

About the Author

Caitlin M.S. Buxbaum is a writer, teacher, visual artist and coach from Wasilla, Alaska. She has a Master of Arts in Teaching from the University of Alaska Anchorage and a Bachelor of Arts in Japanese and English with an emphasis in Creative Writing from Gustavus Adolphus College. This is her first book.

Other Books by Caitlin M. S. Buxbaum

Ever Unknown, Ever Misunderstood

Uneven Lanes

Wabi-Sabi World: An Artist's Search

Follow the author on Facebook, Instagram and Twitter @caitbuxbaum or visit her website: caitbuxbaum.com. In addition to Amazon, you can buy her books on Smashwords and Blurb.

www.ingramcontent.com/pod-product-compliance
Lightning Source LLC
Chambersburg PA
CBHW041814040426
42450CB00004B/152